K. CONNORS

Taylor Swift Biography

From Country Roots to Global Pop Icon, Songwriting Mastery, and Inspiring Activism

This book was professionally typeset on Reedsy.
Find out more at reedsy.com

Contents

Contents

Introduction: The Phenomenon of Taylor Swift

When you think of modern music icons, Taylor Swift is likely one of the first names that comes to mind. She's a force of nature in the music industry, a name synonymous with catchy tunes, heartfelt lyrics, and a seemingly endless string of hits. But Taylor Swift is more than just a pop star—she's a cultural phenomenon, a trendsetter, and an artist who has managed to evolve with the times while staying true to her roots.

Born in Reading, Pennsylvania, and raised in the nearby town of Wyomissing, Taylor Alison Swift always seemed destined for greatness. From a young age, she exhibited a passion for music and a talent for storytelling. Her ability to weave personal experiences into her songs has been a hallmark of her career, creating a deep connection with her fans. This connection is one of the key elements that set her apart from many of her contemporaries.

Taylor's journey to stardom began in Nashville, Tennessee, the heart of country music. At just 14 years old, she moved to Music City with her family, determined to break into the industry. It's worth noting that this move wasn't just a whim—it was a calculated step driven by her unwavering ambition and the support of her family, particularly her mother, Andrea. This early move to Nashville is a testament to her dedication and the strong support system she had from the beginning.

In Nashville, Taylor began honing her craft, performing at local venues and networking with industry professionals. Her hard work paid off when she signed with Big Machine Records and released her self-titled debut album in 2006. This album was a critical and commercial success, establishing her as a rising star in country music. Songs like "Tim McGraw" and "Teardrops on My Guitar" resonated with a young audience, many of whom were experiencing the trials and tribulations of teenage life just like Taylor.

One of the remarkable aspects of Taylor Swift's career is her ability to evolve. With her second album, "Fearless," she didn't just stick to the same formula— she expanded her sound and her audience. The album featured hit singles like "Love Story" and "You Belong with Me," which showcased her knack for catchy hooks and relatable lyrics. "Fearless" was a massive success, earning Taylor her first Grammy Awards, including the coveted Album of the Year.

Taylor's shift from country to pop was a bold move, but it was one that paid off handsomely. With her 2012 album "Red," she began to incorporate more pop elements into her music. This album marked a significant turning point in her career, featuring a mix of country, pop, and rock influences. Songs like "We Are Never Ever Getting Back Together" and "I Knew You Were Trouble" became anthems for a generation, and the album's success solidified her status as a crossover artist.

The release of "1989" in 2014 marked Taylor's full-fledged transition to pop. This album was a game-changer, both for her career and for the music industry. It was critically acclaimed and commercially successful, spawning hits like "Shake It Off," "Blank Space," and "Bad Blood." "1989" won the Grammy Award for Album of the Year, making Taylor the first woman to win this award twice. The album's success also highlighted her ability to reinvent herself while maintaining her core identity.

Throughout her career, Taylor Swift has been known for her songwriting prowess. She writes or co-writes almost all of her songs, and her lyrics often draw from her own experiences. This personal touch gives her music an authenticity that resonates with listeners. Whether she's singing about heartbreak, friendship, or personal growth, her songs have a way of making you feel like she's speaking directly to you. This connection is a big part of why she has such a loyal and passionate fanbase.

Taylor's influence extends beyond music. She's also known for her philanthropy and activism. Over the years, she has donated millions of dollars to various causes, including education, disaster relief, and LGBTQ+ rights. She has also used her platform to speak out on important social and political issues. For example, she has been vocal about the importance of voting and has encouraged her fans to participate in the political process. Her willingness to use her voice for good has earned her respect and admiration from fans and peers alike.

One of the more recent chapters in Taylor's career is her battle for control over her master recordings. In 2019, it was revealed that her former record label, Big Machine, had sold her master recordings to a private equity firm without her consent. This sparked a public feud and brought attention to the issue of artists' rights in the music industry. In response, Taylor decided to re-record her first six albums, a move that has been praised as a bold stand for artists' control over their work.

Taylor Swift's ability to adapt and reinvent herself has been key to her longevity in the music industry. From her early days as a country music prodigy to her current status as a pop superstar, she has continually evolved while staying true to her core values and artistic vision. Her journey is a testament to the power of hard work, resilience, and staying true to oneself.

As we dive into the various chapters of her life and career, we'll explore the highs and lows, the triumphs and challenges, and the lessons that can be learned from her incredible journey. Whether you're a die-hard Swiftie or just a casual fan, there's something to be gained from understanding the story of Taylor Swift. Her ability to connect with people through her music, her resilience in the face of adversity, and her willingness to stand up for what she believes in make her a truly remarkable figure in modern music and culture.

Chapter 1: Early Life and Roots

Taylor Alison Swift was born on December 13, 1989, in Reading, Pennsylvania, a city known more for its industrial history than for producing pop icons. However, from a young age, it was clear that Taylor was no ordinary child. She was raised in the small town of Wyomissing, Pennsylvania, where her love for music and storytelling began to flourish. Her parents, Scott and Andrea Swift, played significant roles in nurturing her talents and dreams, ensuring she had the support she needed to pursue her passion.

Taylor's family had a unique dynamic that contributed to her early development as an artist. Her father, Scott, was a financial advisor, and her mother, Andrea, worked as a mutual fund marketing executive before becoming a full-time mom. Taylor's younger brother, Austin, also showed creative inclinations, although his path would eventually lead him to acting. Growing up, Taylor was surrounded by a loving and supportive family environment, which provided a stable foundation for her burgeoning career.

From an early age, Taylor showed an interest in the arts. She would perform in school plays, sing in the church choir, and participate in local talent shows. Her grandmother, Majorie Finlay, was an opera singer, and Taylor often cited her as a significant influence. The stories of her grandmother's performances and the power of music to move and inspire people left a lasting impression on young Taylor.

At just nine years old, Taylor began performing at local festivals and fairs, showcasing her talent for singing and playing the guitar. These early performances were a mix of covers and original songs, highlighting her ability to connect with audiences through her music. Taylor's natural stage presence and confidence were evident even at this young age, setting her apart from other aspiring musicians in her community.

One of the key turning points in Taylor's early life came when she discovered country music. She was captivated by the storytelling aspect of the genre and the emotional depth of the songs. Artists like Shania Twain, Faith Hill, and LeAnn Rimes became her idols, and she began to emulate their style and sound. Taylor's love for country music was more than just a phase; it became a defining element of her artistic identity.

Recognizing her daughter's talent and dedication, Andrea Swift took an active role in Taylor's early career. She would drive Taylor to Nashville, the heart of country music, where they would hand out demo CDs and meet with industry professionals. These trips were not only an opportunity for Taylor to showcase her talent but also a chance for her to immerse herself in the culture and community of country music.

Taylor's big break came when she performed at Nashville's iconic Bluebird Cafe. This performance caught the attention of Scott Borchetta, a record executive who was in the process of starting his own label, Big Machine Records. Impressed by Taylor's talent and potential, Borchetta signed her as one of the label's first artists. This was a pivotal moment in Taylor's career, providing her with the platform she needed to launch her music on a larger scale.

While Nashville played a crucial role in shaping Taylor's career, her roots in Pennsylvania were equally important. Growing up in Wyomissing, Taylor was influenced by the small-town values and close-knit community that surrounded her. These influences are evident in her early songwriting, which often reflects themes of love, family, and personal growth. Taylor's ability to draw from her own experiences and environment added an authenticity to her music that resonated with listeners.

One of the first songs that Taylor wrote was "Lucky You," a song about a woman who is thankful for the love and support she receives from her partner. Although it was never officially released, the song demonstrated Taylor's early talent for crafting heartfelt lyrics and melodies. This knack for songwriting would become a hallmark of her career, setting her apart from many of her peers in the music industry.

As Taylor continued to hone her craft, she began to develop a distinctive style that blended traditional country elements with modern pop influences. This fusion of genres allowed her to appeal to a broad audience, bridging the gap between country and pop music. Taylor's ability to navigate these two worlds was a testament to her versatility and creativity as an artist.

In addition to her musical talents, Taylor's early years were marked by a strong sense of determination and work ethic. She was known for her relentless drive and willingness to put in the hours needed to achieve her goals. Whether it was practicing guitar for hours on end or writing songs late into the night, Taylor's commitment to her craft was unwavering. This dedication would serve her well as she navigated the challenges and opportunities of the music industry.

Taylor's move to Nashville at the age of 14 was a significant step in her journey. It was a bold decision, reflecting her and her family's belief in her potential. In Nashville, Taylor attended Hendersonville High School while continuing to pursue her music career. Balancing school and music was no easy feat, but Taylor managed to excel in both areas. Her time in Nashville allowed her to immerse herself in the music scene, learn from seasoned professionals, and build the connections that would be crucial to her success.

During her early years in Nashville, Taylor wrote and recorded a number of songs that would later become part of her debut album. She worked with experienced songwriters like Liz Rose, who helped her refine her ideas and develop her unique voice. This period of collaboration and growth was essential in shaping Taylor's artistic identity and preparing her for the next phase of her career.

Taylor's self-titled debut album, released in 2006, was a culmination of years of hard work and dedication. The album featured a mix of country and pop songs, showcasing Taylor's versatility and broad appeal. Tracks like "Tim McGraw," "Teardrops on My Guitar," and "Our Song" quickly became hits, establishing Taylor as a rising star in the music industry. Her ability to connect with listeners through her music was evident from the start, and the success of her debut album laid the foundation for her future achievements.

The release of Taylor's debut album marked the beginning of a new chapter in her life. She transitioned from a small-town girl with big dreams to a nationally recognized artist with a growing fanbase. However, despite her early success, Taylor remained grounded and focused on her goals. She continued to write and record new music, always striving to improve and evolve as an artist.

Taylor's early life and roots played a crucial role in shaping her career and artistic identity. The support of her family, the influence of her hometown, and the lessons she learned in Nashville all contributed to her success. Taylor's journey from Wyomissing to Nashville was marked by hard work, determination, and a relentless pursuit of her dreams. As she continued to grow and evolve as an artist, these early experiences would remain a foundational part of her story, influencing her music and inspiring her fans around the world.

Chapter 2: The Nashville Dream

Taylor Swift's journey to becoming one of the biggest names in music began in the heart of country music: Nashville, Tennessee. But before we dive into her Nashville years, let's rewind a bit to understand the roots that shaped her early ambitions.

Taylor was born on December 13, 1989, in Reading, Pennsylvania, but she spent her formative years in the small town of Wyomissing. Her parents, Scott and Andrea Swift, were supportive and nurturing, fostering an environment where her budding talents could thrive. Taylor's love for music was evident from a young age. She was particularly drawn to storytelling, which is a hallmark of country music. By the time she was 10, she was performing at local events, fairs, and contests, showcasing a precocious talent that set her apart from her peers.

The Swifts were not a typical musical family, but they recognized Taylor's potential and were willing to make significant sacrifices to support her dreams. Andrea, especially, played a pivotal role in Taylor's early career, managing her schedule, driving her to auditions, and helping her navigate the often daunting music industry landscape.

The move to Nashville was a calculated and strategic decision. At just 14 years old, Taylor convinced her parents to relocate to the country music capital. This move wasn't just about finding better opportunities—it was about immersing herself in the culture and community that would become the foundation of her career. Nashville, with its rich history and vibrant music scene, was the perfect place for a young artist with big dreams.

In Nashville, Taylor quickly immersed herself in the music scene. She began performing at iconic venues like the Bluebird Cafe, where many country legends got their start. These performances were not just about showcasing her talent—they were about networking and getting noticed by the right people. Taylor's ability to connect with audiences, even at such a young age, made her stand out. Her songs were a mix of youthful innocence and profound insight, resonating with people of all ages.

One of the key figures in Taylor's early career was Scott Borchetta, the founder of Big Machine Records. Borchetta saw something special in Taylor and signed her to his newly formed label. This partnership was a turning point. It provided Taylor with the resources and support she needed to take her career to the next level.

Taylor's self-titled debut album, released in 2006, was a mix of country and pop, featuring songs that she had written herself. This album wasn't just a showcase of her musical talent—it was a testament to her songwriting abilities. Tracks like "Tim McGraw" and "Teardrops on My Guitar" were not only commercially successful but also critically acclaimed. They highlighted Taylor's knack for storytelling and her ability to capture the complexities of teenage life in a way that was both relatable and poignant.

"Tim McGraw," in particular, was a clever move. By naming her debut single after a country music icon, Taylor immediately aligned herself with the genre's greats while also paying homage to an artist who had influenced her. The song is a nostalgic reflection on a past relationship, showcasing her ability to blend personal experiences with universal themes. This approach became a hallmark of her music, endearing her to fans who felt she was singing about their own lives.

The success of her debut album catapulted Taylor into the spotlight, but she didn't rest on her laurels. She was determined to build on this momentum and establish herself as a formidable force in the music industry. Her follow-up album, "Fearless," released in 2008, was a critical and commercial triumph. It solidified her status as a rising star and earned her numerous accolades, including her first Grammy Awards.

Nashville wasn't just a backdrop for Taylor's rise to fame—it was a vital part of her story. The city's culture, history, and community played a significant role in shaping her as an artist. From the honky-tonks on Broadway to the recording studios on Music Row, Nashville's influence is evident in every note of Taylor's early music.

One of the things that set Taylor apart in the Nashville scene was her work ethic. She was not content to simply be a performer; she wanted to be involved in every aspect of her career. She co-wrote almost all the songs on her debut album and continued to do so on subsequent albums. This hands-on approach gave her music an authenticity and personal touch that resonated with fans.

Another significant aspect of Taylor's early career was her use of social media. At a time when many artists were still figuring out how to connect with fans online, Taylor was a pioneer. She used platforms like MySpace to interact with her fans, share updates, and build a community. This direct connection with her audience was a key factor in her early success and helped her build a loyal fanbase that has followed her throughout her career.

Taylor's time in Nashville also taught her valuable lessons about the music industry. She learned the importance of networking, the value of hard work, and the necessity of staying true to oneself. These lessons would serve her well as she navigated the ups and downs of her career.

But perhaps one of the most important takeaways from Taylor's Nashville years is the power of perseverance. Breaking into the music industry is no easy feat, and it often involves a lot of rejection and setbacks. Taylor faced her fair share of challenges, but she never gave up. Her determination, combined with her talent and hard work, eventually paid off, paving the way for a career that has spanned more than a decade and shows no signs of slowing down.

The story of Taylor Swift's early years in Nashville is not just about a young girl chasing her dreams—it's about the making of an artist who would go on to redefine the music industry. Her experiences in Nashville laid the foundation for her future success and helped shape her into the powerhouse she is today. From her first performances at the Bluebird Cafe to her breakout debut album, Nashville was the proving ground where Taylor honed her craft and built the career that would make her a global superstar.

Chapter 3: Fearless and Rising Fame

By the time Taylor Swift released her second album, "Fearless," in 2008, she was already on the cusp of stardom. Her self-titled debut had introduced her to the world as a fresh, young voice in country music. But "Fearless" was the album that would catapult her into the stratosphere, transforming her from a promising newcomer into a bona fide superstar. This chapter of her career is a fascinating study in how an artist can capture the zeitgeist and, in doing so, redefine an entire genre.

"Fearless" was an apt title for the album, reflecting not just the themes of the songs but also Taylor's approach to her music and career. She took bold risks, both sonically and lyrically, that paid off in spectacular fashion. The album was a critical and commercial triumph, earning her multiple awards, including four Grammy Awards, and cementing her status as a rising star.

One of the standout tracks on "Fearless" is "Love Story," a song that has become synonymous with Taylor Swift. This modern-day fairy tale reimagines the classic Romeo and Juliet story with a happy ending, a stark contrast to Shakespeare's tragic conclusion. The song's catchy melody and relatable lyrics struck a chord with listeners, making it one of Taylor's most enduring hits. "Love Story" showcased her ability to blend country and pop elements seamlessly, appealing to a broad audience while staying true to her roots.

Another significant track from "Fearless" is "You Belong with Me." This song, with its infectious hook and high school romance storyline, became an anthem for many young fans. The music video, featuring Taylor in dual roles as both the girl-next-door and the popular cheerleader, further cemented her relatable image. "You Belong with Me" exemplifies Taylor's knack for capturing the universal experiences of teenage life, turning them into sing-along moments that resonate across generations.

The success of "Fearless" wasn't just about catchy singles; it was also about Taylor's growth as a songwriter. She co-wrote all the songs on the album, drawing from her own experiences and emotions. Tracks like "White Horse" and "Fifteen" delve into the complexities of young love and heartbreak with a maturity beyond her years. "White Horse," for instance, is a poignant ballad about the disillusionment of a failed relationship, showcasing Taylor's ability to convey deep emotion through her music.

"Fifteen," on the other hand, is a reflective look at the innocence and naivety of adolescence. In the song, Taylor reminisces about her freshman year of high school, capturing the bittersweet nature of growing up. This song is particularly notable for its introspective lyrics and the way it encourages listeners to cherish their youthful experiences while learning from them.

The "Fearless" era also marked Taylor's first major foray into international stardom. Her appeal crossed borders and cultures, resonating with fans worldwide. The album's success was bolstered by an extensive tour that saw Taylor performing to sold-out arenas across the globe. The Fearless Tour was not just a series of concerts; it was a meticulously crafted spectacle that showcased Taylor's talents as a performer and entertainer. Her ability to connect with audiences, whether through intimate acoustic sets or full-blown stage productions, was a key factor in her rising fame.

In addition to her musical achievements, Taylor began to make a significant impact on the broader cultural landscape. She was becoming a fashion icon, known for her distinctive style that blended classic elegance with modern trends. Her red carpet appearances were closely watched, and she graced the covers of numerous magazines. This visibility helped her reach an even wider audience, making her a household name.

Taylor's influence extended beyond music and fashion. She began to use her platform to advocate for issues she cared about, setting the stage for her future activism. During the "Fearless" era, she was particularly vocal about the importance of education and literacy, donating books to schools and libraries across the country. Her philanthropic efforts earned her praise and solidified her reputation as a role model for young fans.

The critical acclaim for "Fearless" was substantial. The album received numerous awards, including the Grammy for Album of the Year, making Taylor the youngest artist to win this prestigious honor at the time. This recognition from the music industry was a validation of her talent and hard work, and it paved the way for future successes.

One of the more memorable moments from this period was Taylor's acceptance speech at the 2009 MTV Video Music Awards, which was famously interrupted by Kanye West. This incident, while shocking at the time, became a pivotal moment in pop culture. It highlighted the challenges Taylor faced as a young woman navigating the complexities of fame, and it ultimately showcased her grace under pressure. The incident also sparked a broader conversation about respect and recognition in the music industry.

Despite the challenges and controversies, the "Fearless" era was overwhelmingly positive for Taylor. It was a time of significant growth and achievement, both personally and professionally. She demonstrated an uncanny ability to connect with fans, write compelling songs, and handle the pressures of fame with maturity and poise.

Looking back, "Fearless" stands as a testament to Taylor Swift's talent and determination. It was an album that not only solidified her place in the music industry but also set the stage for future evolution. The themes of love, heartbreak, and personal growth explored in "Fearless" would continue to be central to her music, but with each new album, she would push the boundaries further, exploring new sounds and ideas.

As we move forward in her career, we'll see how the lessons learned and successes achieved during the "Fearless" era would influence her subsequent projects. Taylor Swift's ability to reinvent herself while staying true to her core identity is one of the reasons she has remained relevant and beloved by fans for over a decade. The "Fearless" chapter of her story is a reminder that taking risks, staying authentic, and connecting with people on a personal level are essential ingredients for lasting success.

Chapter 4: Redefining Pop with "Red"

By the time Taylor Swift began working on her fourth studio album, "Red," she had already established herself as a formidable force in the country music world. However, Taylor was never one to rest on her laurels. With "Red," released in 2012, she took bold steps to expand her musical horizons, pushing the boundaries of her sound and redefining her image. This chapter in her career is a fascinating exploration of an artist in transition, embracing new influences and experimenting with different styles.

"Red" is often described as a transitional album, and for good reason. It marked a significant departure from Taylor's earlier country roots, incorporating a diverse range of musical genres, including pop, rock, and electronic elements. The album's eclectic sound was a reflection of Taylor's evolving musical tastes and her desire to reach a broader audience. She collaborated with a variety of producers and songwriters, including Max Martin, Shellback, and Ed Sheeran, who brought their own distinct flavors to the project.

One of the standout tracks from "Red" is "We Are Never Ever Getting Back Together," a pop anthem that became an instant hit. The song's catchy melody, infectious chorus, and sassy lyrics made it a fan favorite and a commercial success. It was also a clear indication of Taylor's shift towards a more pop-oriented sound. The song's production, characterized by its polished, radio-friendly sheen, was a departure from the more organic, country-influenced arrangements of her previous work.

"We Are Never Ever Getting Back Together" also showcased Taylor's sharp wit and storytelling prowess. The song's lyrics, which recount a tumultuous on-again, off-again relationship, resonated with many listeners who had experienced similar romantic rollercoasters. The track's playful tone and memorable hook made it a standout moment in Taylor's discography and a defining song of the "Red" era.

Another key track from the album is "I Knew You Were Trouble," which further demonstrated Taylor's willingness to experiment with new sounds. The song features a dubstep-inspired drop, a surprising and bold choice that caught many fans and critics off guard. This genre-blending approach was indicative of Taylor's fearlessness as an artist, unafraid to take risks and challenge expectations. "I Knew You Were Trouble" became another major hit, cementing Taylor's status as a pop innovator.

The title track, "Red," is a perfect example of the album's thematic depth and emotional complexity. The song uses the color red as a metaphor for intense, passionate love and the heartbreak that often accompanies it. Taylor's vivid imagery and evocative lyrics paint a picture of a love that is both exhilarating and destructive. The track's blend of country and rock elements creates a dynamic soundscape that perfectly complements the song's lyrical content.

One of the more intimate and introspective moments on the album is "All Too Well." Widely regarded as one of Taylor's best songs, "All Too Well" is a deeply personal ballad that recounts the memories of a past relationship with heartbreaking detail. The song's emotional intensity and raw honesty resonated with many fans, who appreciated Taylor's willingness to share her vulnerabilities. "All Too Well" is a testament to Taylor's strength as a songwriter, capable of capturing complex emotions with precision and nuance.

"Red" also features several notable collaborations. "Everything Has Changed," a duet with Ed Sheeran, is a sweet and tender song about the transformative power of love. The chemistry between Taylor and Ed is palpable, and their vocal harmonies add a layer of warmth and sincerity to the track. Another standout collaboration is "The Last Time," featuring Gary Lightbody of Snow Patrol. This haunting duet explores the themes of love and regret, with Taylor and Gary's voices blending beautifully over a somber, orchestral arrangement.

The success of "Red" was not limited to its commercial performance; it also received critical acclaim. Many reviewers praised Taylor's bold artistic choices and her ability to craft a cohesive album despite its stylistic diversity. "Red" was seen as a pivotal moment in Taylor's career, solidifying her reputation as a versatile and innovative artist. The album earned multiple Grammy nominations, including a nod for Album of the Year, further validating Taylor's creative evolution.

The "Red" era also saw Taylor embarking on an ambitious world tour, which showcased her growth as a performer. The Red Tour was a spectacle of lights, costumes, and choreography, reflecting the album's eclectic and vibrant nature. Taylor's stage presence and ability to connect with her audience were on full display, making each concert an unforgettable experience for fans. The tour's success further cemented Taylor's status as a global superstar, capable of commanding arenas and stadiums with ease.

Beyond the music, "Red" marked a period of significant personal growth for Taylor. She navigated the complexities of young adulthood, dealing with the highs and lows of fame, relationships, and self-discovery. The album's themes of love, loss, and resilience resonated with fans who were going through similar experiences. Taylor's openness and authenticity created a deep bond with her audience, who saw her not just as a pop star but as a relatable figure facing the same challenges they did.

The "Red" era also highlighted Taylor's evolving fashion sense. Her style during this period was a mix of classic elegance and modern trends, reflecting her artistic transformation. From her signature red lipstick to her chic, retro-inspired outfits, Taylor's fashion choices became a significant part of her public persona. Her red carpet appearances and magazine covers showcased her as a style icon, influencing trends and inspiring fans worldwide.

"Red" was a turning point in Taylor Swift's career, marking the beginning of her journey towards becoming one of the most influential artists of her generation. The album's innovative sound, compelling lyrics, and emotional depth showcased Taylor's growth as a musician and songwriter. It was a bold statement of artistic intent, proving that she was not afraid to take risks and push the boundaries of her creativity.

As we continue to explore Taylor's career, we'll see how the lessons learned and the successes achieved during the "Red" era paved the way for even greater accomplishments. Taylor Swift's ability to evolve, experiment, and connect with her audience is a testament to her enduring appeal and her unwavering commitment to her craft. The "Red" chapter of her story is a reminder that embracing change and taking risks can lead to some of the most rewarding and transformative moments in an artist's journey.

Chapter 5: "1989" and Global Stardom

With the release of "1989" in 2014, Taylor Swift fully embraced her transformation from country ingénue to pop powerhouse. This album wasn't just a genre shift; it was a bold declaration of independence and artistic evolution. "1989" was an ode to the sounds of the late '80s, infused with modern pop sensibilities, and it marked a new chapter in Taylor's career—one that would propel her to unprecedented global stardom.

The inspiration for "1989" came from a mix of nostalgia and a desire to break free from the constraints of her past work. Taylor has always been an artist deeply connected to her personal experiences, and with this album, she wanted to capture the energy and exuberance of the decade in which she was born. Collaborating with producers like Max Martin, Shellback, and Jack Antonoff, she crafted a collection of songs that were polished, vibrant, and irresistibly catchy.

One of the standout tracks from "1989" is "Shake It Off," a defiant anthem about letting go of negativity and embracing individuality. With its infectious beat and playful lyrics, the song quickly became a massive hit. The accompanying music video, featuring Taylor dancing awkwardly but confidently through various scenarios, was a perfect visual representation of the song's message. "Shake It Off" was more than just a commercial success; it was a cultural phenomenon, cementing Taylor's place in the pop pantheon.

"Blank Space" is another iconic track from the album, showcasing Taylor's ability to poke fun at her own public persona. The song's lyrics playfully address the media's portrayal of her as a serial dater, with Taylor embodying the character of a jilted lover with a penchant for drama. The music video, which features Taylor in a glamorous but unhinged role, adds an extra layer of irony and humor. "Blank Space" was a critical and commercial triumph, further solidifying Taylor's reputation as a master of reinvention.

"1989" also features "Style," a song that perfectly encapsulates the album's retro-modern aesthetic. With its slick production and smooth melodies, "Style" is a celebration of timeless romance. The song's lyrics, rumored to be about Taylor's relationship with Harry Styles, add an element of intrigue and personal connection. The track's lush, shimmering soundscapes reflect Taylor's meticulous attention to detail and her commitment to creating a cohesive sonic experience.

One of the more introspective moments on "1989" is "Out of the Woods," a song co-written with Jack Antonoff. This track, with its driving rhythms and haunting melodies, explores the anxiety and uncertainty of a tumultuous relationship. The repeated refrain, "Are we out of the woods yet?" captures the feeling of being on edge, constantly questioning the stability of the relationship. "Out of the Woods" showcases Taylor's ability to blend personal storytelling with universal themes, making her music resonate with a wide audience.

"1989" wasn't just an album; it was a carefully curated era. Taylor's attention to detail extended beyond the music to every aspect of her public image. From her fashion choices to her social media presence, everything was meticulously planned to align with the album's aesthetic. She adopted a more polished, sophisticated look, often seen in high-waisted skirts, crop tops, and classic red lipstick. This transformation was not just about style but about signaling a new phase in her career—one where she was fully in control of her narrative.

The "1989 World Tour" was a spectacular showcase of Taylor's newfound confidence and global appeal. The tour featured elaborate stage setups, intricate choreography, and a setlist that spanned her entire career. Each concert was a carefully crafted experience, designed to connect with fans on a deep emotional level. Taylor's charisma and stage presence were on full display, proving that she was not just a studio artist but a commanding live performer.

The tour also featured a series of high-profile guest appearances, with celebrities and fellow musicians joining Taylor on stage for memorable performances. These guest spots, dubbed "The Squad," became a talking point in the media, highlighting Taylor's ability to bring people together and create unforgettable moments. This sense of camaraderie and inclusivity was a significant part of the "1989" era, reinforcing Taylor's image as both a pop icon and a relatable figure.

"1989" received widespread critical acclaim, with many reviewers praising Taylor's bold artistic choices and her ability to craft a cohesive, compelling album. The album won several awards, including the Grammy for Album of the Year, making Taylor the first woman to win this award twice. This recognition from the music industry was a testament to her talent, hard work, and vision.

Beyond the accolades, "1989" had a profound impact on pop culture. The album's songs were ubiquitous, dominating radio airwaves and streaming platforms. Taylor's influence extended beyond music, shaping fashion trends and social media conversations. Her ability to connect with fans on a personal level, combined with her savvy use of technology and media, made her one of the most influential figures in the entertainment industry.

The success of "1989" also highlighted Taylor's role as a trailblazer for other artists. Her willingness to take risks and redefine herself inspired many of her peers to push the boundaries of their own music. Taylor's evolution from country star to pop powerhouse demonstrated that it was possible to break free from genre constraints and still achieve massive success. Her journey was a powerful example of how embracing change and taking control of one's narrative can lead to extraordinary achievements.

The "1989" era also marked a significant shift in Taylor's personal life. As she navigated the pressures of fame, she became more vocal about the challenges she faced, including media scrutiny and public perception. Taylor's openness about her experiences resonated with many fans who appreciated her honesty and vulnerability. Her ability to maintain authenticity while navigating the complexities of stardom endeared her to audiences around the world.

"1989" was not just a moment in Taylor Swift's career; it was a milestone in pop music history. The album's innovative sound, memorable visuals, and compelling storytelling set a new standard for what a pop album could be. Taylor's ability to blend nostalgia with contemporary sensibilities created a timeless work that continues to resonate with fans old and new.

As we continue to explore Taylor's journey, we'll see how the lessons learned and the successes achieved during the "1989" era influenced her subsequent projects. Taylor Swift's ability to adapt, innovate, and connect with her audience is a testament to her enduring appeal and her unwavering commitment to her craft. The "1989" chapter of her story is a reminder that true artistry involves not just following trends but setting them and that the most impactful work often comes from taking bold, creative risks.

Chapter 6: Reputation and Reinvention

In 2017, Taylor Swift released her sixth studio album, "Reputation," marking a dramatic shift in her career and public image. This album was a response to the intense media scrutiny and public feuds that had plagued her in the preceding years. With "Reputation," Taylor embraced a darker, edgier persona, using the album as both a personal catharsis and a bold statement of reinvention. This chapter delves into the complexities of "Reputation," exploring its themes, the controversies surrounding it, and its impact on Taylor's career.

The lead-up to "Reputation" was characterized by silence and mystery. After the massive success of "1989," Taylor largely retreated from the public eye. She wiped her social media clean, leaving fans and media alike in suspense. When she finally reemerged, it was with a completely new aesthetic. The first single, "Look What You Made Me Do," was a stark departure from her previous work, featuring a darker, more aggressive tone. The accompanying music video, with its imagery of snakes and references to past controversies, signaled that Taylor was ready to confront her critics head-on.

"Look What You Made Me Do" was a bold and defiant anthem, addressing the various scandals and public disputes that had dominated headlines. The song's chorus, "I'm sorry, the old Taylor can't come to the phone right now. Why? Oh, 'cause she's dead," became an iconic line, symbolizing Taylor's rebirth and reinvention. The song was polarizing, with some praising her boldness and others critiquing the shift in style. However, it undeniably set the tone for the rest of the album.

"Reputation" delves deeply into themes of betrayal, vengeance, and self-empowerment. The album's darker tone and more electronic, synthesized production reflect Taylor's emotional state during its creation. Tracks like "...Ready for It?" and "End Game" showcase a more assertive, confident side of Taylor, embracing a style that blends pop, hip-hop, and electronic influences. The collaborations on these tracks, including features from Ed Sheeran and Future, highlight her willingness to experiment and push the boundaries of her sound.

One of the standout tracks on "Reputation" is "Delicate," which offers a more vulnerable glimpse into Taylor's emotional landscape. The song explores the fragility of new love amidst a backdrop of intense public scrutiny. Its softer, more melodic tone contrasts with the album's overall darker aesthetic, showcasing Taylor's versatility as a songwriter. "Delicate" resonated with many fans, who appreciated its honest and introspective lyrics.

Another notable song is "Getaway Car," which narrates the story of a doomed romance, likened to a heist gone wrong. The track's driving beat and cinematic lyrics make it a standout moment on the album. "Getaway Car" is a masterclass in storytelling, weaving together themes of escape, betrayal, and inevitable downfall. It's a reminder of Taylor's ability to craft compelling narratives within her music, even amidst an album centered on personal reinvention.

The theme of reputation is central to the album, and nowhere is it more evident than in the track "This Is Why We Can't Have Nice Things." This song is a direct response to her public fallout with Kanye West and Kim Kardashian, addressing the betrayal and mockery she felt. With its playful, sarcastic tone, the song highlights Taylor's ability to use humor and wit to address serious subjects. It's a cathartic moment on the album, providing insight into how she processed and overcame these public disputes.

"Reputation" also features moments of genuine romance and affection, particularly in songs like "Call It What You Want" and "New Year's Day." These tracks offer a glimpse into Taylor's personal life and her relationship with British actor Joe Alwyn. "Call It What You Want" is a tender love song that emphasizes the importance of finding stability and trust in a relationship, despite the chaos of the outside world. "New Year's Day," the closing track of the album, is a poignant, stripped-down ballad that reflects on the beauty of everyday moments shared with a loved one. These songs provide a counterbalance to the album's darker themes, showcasing the multifaceted nature of Taylor's emotions and experiences.

The "Reputation" era was not just about the music; it was a complete rebranding. Taylor's fashion evolved to match the album's aesthetic, featuring edgier, bolder looks. Her public appearances and performances were carefully curated to reinforce the themes of the album. The "Reputation Stadium Tour" was a spectacular production, featuring elaborate sets, pyrotechnics, and choreography that brought the album's songs to life. The tour was a massive success, breaking records and demonstrating Taylor's prowess as a live performer.

Critically, "Reputation" received mixed reviews, with some praising its boldness and innovation, while others were less receptive to its darker tone and departure from her earlier work. However, commercially, the album was a triumph, debuting at number one on the Billboard 200 and selling over a million copies in its first week. The success of "Reputation" underscored Taylor's ability to defy expectations and maintain her relevance in an ever-changing music landscape.

Beyond the commercial and critical reception, "Reputation" had a profound impact on Taylor's career and personal life. The album's themes of reinvention and self-empowerment resonated with many fans who had followed her journey from her country roots to pop superstardom. "Reputation" marked a turning point, not just in her music, but in how she managed her public image and dealt with personal adversity.

The creation of "Reputation" also highlighted Taylor's resilience and determination. Faced with intense media scrutiny and public challenges, she used her art to process and transcend these experiences. The album is a testament to her strength and ability to turn adversity into creative fuel. It demonstrated that Taylor was not just a pop star but an artist with depth, capable of evolving and pushing her boundaries.

The "Reputation" era also paved the way for a more open and candid Taylor. In subsequent interviews and public appearances, she began to speak more openly about her struggles and the lessons she had learned. This newfound transparency endeared her to fans even more, as they saw her not just as a distant celebrity but as a relatable figure navigating the complexities of life and fame.

"Reputation" is a pivotal chapter in Taylor Swift's career, marking a period of profound change and growth. It is an album that challenged both her and her audience, pushing the boundaries of what was expected from her music and persona. Through its bold themes, innovative sound, and unflinching honesty, "Reputation" stands as a testament to Taylor's artistry and resilience. It set the stage for the next phase of her career, where she would continue to evolve, experiment, and redefine herself, always staying true to her core as a storyteller and musician.

Chapter 7: Lover and Embracing Positivity

Following the intense and brooding era of "Reputation," Taylor Swift's next chapter was marked by a significant shift in tone and theme. With the release of "Lover" in 2019, Taylor embraced a lighter, more colorful aesthetic, celebrating love, joy, and personal growth. This chapter explores the creation and impact of "Lover," examining how Taylor's renewed focus on positivity influenced her music and public persona.

"Lover" was a breath of fresh air, both for Taylor and her fans. After the darkness of "Reputation," the album's pastel-colored visuals and uplifting messages were a welcome change. The title track, "Lover," is a tender, heartfelt ballad that captures the essence of the album. With its romantic lyrics and nostalgic feel, the song quickly became a favorite among fans. "Lover" showcases Taylor's ability to craft intimate, personal songs that resonate on a universal level.

The lead single, "ME!" featuring Brendon Urie of Panic! At The Disco, set the tone for the album. "ME!" is a vibrant, exuberant anthem celebrating individuality and self-love. The song's catchy chorus and playful lyrics made it an instant hit, and its colorful, whimsical music video reflected the album's overall aesthetic. "ME!" was a stark departure from the darker, more introspective songs on "Reputation," signaling a new, more positive phase in Taylor's career.

"YNTCD" (You Need to Calm Down), another standout track from "Lover," is a bold, defiant anthem promoting acceptance and equality. The song addresses online trolls and homophobia with a witty, tongue-in-cheek approach, emphasizing the importance of kindness and understanding. The music video features a star-studded cast, including several prominent LGBTQ+ celebrities, and ends with a powerful call for equality. "YNTCD" was praised for its message and became an anthem for the LGBTQ+ community, further cementing Taylor's role as an advocate for social issues.

The album "Lover" is rich with a variety of musical styles and themes, showcasing Taylor's versatility as an artist. "The Archer" is a hauntingly beautiful track that delves into feelings of vulnerability and self-doubt. Its ethereal production and introspective lyrics highlight Taylor's ability to explore complex emotions with depth and nuance. "The Archer" is a reminder that even in a predominantly positive album, Taylor doesn't shy away from addressing the darker aspects of the human experience.

"Miss Americana & The Heartbreak Prince" is a standout track that blends political commentary with a high school romance metaphor. The song reflects Taylor's growing political consciousness and her willingness to address societal issues through her music. Its cinematic production and vivid storytelling make it one of the most compelling songs on the album, offering a glimpse into Taylor's evolving worldview.

"Paper Rings" is a fun, upbeat track that captures the joy and spontaneity of love. With its catchy melody and playful lyrics, the song is a celebration of finding happiness in the simple things. "Paper Rings" showcases Taylor's talent for writing infectious pop songs that are both lighthearted and mean-ingful. It's a testament to her ability to infuse joy into her music, creating moments of pure happiness for her listeners.

The track "Cornelia Street" is a nostalgic ode to a specific place and the memories associated with it. The song's detailed lyrics and emotional delivery create a vivid picture of a past relationship, highlighting Taylor's storytelling prowess. "Cornelia Street" is a reminder of the power of place and memory in shaping our experiences and emotions. It's a beautifully crafted song that resonates with anyone who has ever been deeply connected to a particular location.

One of the more poignant moments on "Lover" is "Soon You'll Get Better," a collaboration with the Dixie Chicks (now known as The Chicks). The song addresses Taylor's mother's battle with cancer, offering a raw and emotional look at her family's struggles. "Soon You'll Get Better" is a deeply personal track, and its inclusion on the album highlights Taylor's willingness to share her most vulnerable moments with her audience. The song's heartfelt lyrics and stripped-down production make it one of the most moving tracks in Taylor's discography.

The "Lover" era also saw Taylor taking a more active role in political and social advocacy. She publicly endorsed political candidates for the first time, encouraging her fans to vote and get involved in the political process. This newfound activism was a significant shift for Taylor, who had previously been more private about her political views. Her willingness to speak out on important issues resonated with many fans, who appreciated her using her platform for positive change.

The "Lover Fest" was planned as a series of festival-style concerts to celebrate the album, but the COVID-19 pandemic forced Taylor to cancel the tour. Despite this setback, the "Lover" era remained a period of joy and creativity. Taylor's engagement with her fans through social media and virtual events helped maintain a sense of connection and community, even in challenging times.

"Lover" was both a critical and commercial success, debuting at number one on the Billboard 200 and receiving widespread acclaim. Critics praised the album's diverse musical styles and its optimistic, heartfelt themes. "Lover" showcased Taylor's ability to continually evolve as an artist, embracing new sounds and ideas while staying true to her core as a storyteller.

The "Lover" era also marked a significant moment in Taylor's personal life. Her relationship with Joe Alwyn, which had been relatively private, became a source of inspiration for many of the album's love songs. Taylor's happiness and contentment during this period were evident in her music, reflecting a sense of peace and fulfillment that resonated with her fans.

"Lover" is a celebration of love in all its forms—romantic, self-love, and love for friends and family. It's an album that embraces positivity and joy, offering a refreshing contrast to the darker themes of "Reputation." Through its vibrant, colorful aesthetic and heartfelt lyrics, "Lover" captures the essence of finding happiness and embracing the beauty of life.

The "Lover" chapter of Taylor Swift's career is a testament to her ability to reinvent herself and find new ways to connect with her audience. It's a reminder that even in the face of adversity, there's always room for hope, joy, and love. The album's themes of positivity and personal growth resonate deeply, offering a message of resilience and optimism that continues to inspire fans around the world. As we move forward in Taylor's journey, we'll see how the lessons and experiences of the "Lover" era influence her future work, shaping her ever-evolving artistic path.

Chapter 8: Folklore and Evermore – The Surprise Albums

In 2020, amid a global pandemic that brought much of the world to a standstill, Taylor Swift did what she does best: she surprised everyone. In a year marked by uncertainty and isolation, Taylor released not one, but two albums— "Folklore" and "Evermore"—both of which marked a dramatic shift in her musical style and lyrical approach. These surprise albums, announced with little warning, offered a deep, introspective dive into storytelling and stripped-down, folk-inspired sounds. This chapter explores the creation, themes, and impact of "Folklore" and "Evermore," and how they represented a bold artistic departure for Taylor Swift.

"Folklore," released in July 2020, was a departure from the bright, pop-centric sound of "Lover." Instead, it embraced a more subdued, introspective style, drawing heavily from indie folk, alternative rock, and lo-fi influences. The album was created in collaboration with Aaron Dessner of The National, Jack Antonoff, and Bon Iver's Justin Vernon. The collaboration with Dessner, in particular, brought a new texture to Taylor's music, infusing it with a layered, atmospheric quality that was both haunting and beautiful.

The lead single, "Cardigan," set the tone for the album. It is a tender, melancholic song that weaves together themes of lost love and nostalgia. The song's lyrics are rich with imagery and metaphors, showcasing Taylor's growth as a storyteller. The music video, directed by Taylor herself, features dreamlike visuals that complement the song's introspective mood. "Cardigan" quickly became a fan favorite, highlighting the emotional depth and artistic maturity of the album.

"Folklore" is an album that thrives on narrative complexity and character-driven songs. "The Last Great American Dynasty" is a prime example of this. The song tells the story of Rebekah Harkness, the former owner of Taylor's Rhode Island home, blending historical details with Taylor's personal reflections. The song's clever storytelling and catchy melody make it a standout track, illustrating Taylor's ability to create vivid, compelling narratives.

Another highlight is "Exile," a duet with Bon Iver. This song is a hauntingly beautiful exploration of a failed relationship, with Taylor and Justin Vernon's voices blending seamlessly over a minimalist piano arrangement. "Exile" captures the pain and confusion of a breakup, with each singer offering a different perspective on the dissolution of the relationship. The song's raw emotion and stark arrangement make it one of the most powerful moments on the album.

"Folklore" also delves into themes of escapism and self-reflection. Songs like "Seven" and "August" evoke a sense of longing and nostalgia, capturing the bittersweet nature of memory and the passage of time. "Seven" is a delicate, almost childlike song that reflects on the innocence of childhood friendships, while "August" is a wistful look at a fleeting summer romance. Both songs showcase Taylor's lyrical prowess and her ability to evoke deep emotions with subtle, evocative imagery.

"The 1," the album's opening track, sets the stage for the introspective journey that follows. It is a reflective song about missed opportunities and what-ifs, blending a wistful tone with a sense of acceptance. The song's understated production and contemplative lyrics immediately draw listeners into the world of "Folklore," setting the tone for the rest of the album.

"Folklore" was met with widespread critical acclaim, with many reviewers praising its mature songwriting and cohesive sound. The album debuted at number one on the Billboard 200, becoming Taylor's seventh consecutive album to achieve this feat. It also earned several Grammy nominations, including Album of the Year, which it won. This recognition from the music industry was a testament to Taylor's ability to continually evolve as an artist and push the boundaries of her creativity.

Just five months after the release of "Folklore," Taylor surprised fans again with the release of "Evermore," described as the sister album to "Folklore." While "Evermore" continued in the same folk-inspired vein, it also expanded on the themes and sounds introduced in "Folklore." The album featured collaborations with many of the same artists, including Aaron Dessner, Jack Antonoff, and Justin Vernon, as well as new collaborators like HAIM.

"Willow," the lead single from "Evermore," is a mystical, enchanting song that explores themes of love and fate. The song's ethereal production and poetic lyrics make it a perfect continuation of the world established in "Folklore." The music video, which picks up where the "Cardigan" video left off, further emphasizes the interconnectedness of the two albums.

"Evermore" is rich with storytelling and character-driven songs. "Tis the Damn Season" and "Dorothea" are two interconnected tracks that tell the story of a woman returning to her hometown and reconnecting with a past lover. "Tis the Damn Season" is told from the woman's perspective, capturing the bittersweet emotions of revisiting old memories, while "Dorothea" provides the perspective of the lover left behind. These songs highlight Taylor's ability to create multi-faceted characters and weave their stories together in a meaningful way.

"Champagne Problems" is another standout track, exploring the aftermath of a broken engagement. The song's poignant lyrics and delicate piano arrangement create a sense of intimacy and heartbreak. "Champagne Problems" is a masterclass in storytelling, with Taylor painting a vivid picture of love, regret, and missed opportunities.

"Evermore" also features moments of whimsy and fantasy. "Gold Rush," co-written with Jack Antonoff, is a dreamy, almost surreal song that explores themes of desire and unattainable beauty. The song's lush production and poetic lyrics make it a captivating listen, showcasing Taylor's ability to blend fantasy and reality in her music.

One of the most powerful tracks on "Evermore" is "Marjorie," a tribute to Taylor's late grandmother. The song reflects on the lessons and memories Taylor has from her grandmother, blending personal anecdotes with universal themes of loss and remembrance. "Marjorie" is a deeply emotional song that resonates with anyone who has experienced the loss of a loved one, highlighting Taylor's gift for writing songs that touch on deeply personal yet universally relatable experiences.

The title track, "Evermore," featuring Bon Iver, is a fitting conclusion to the album. The song is a meditative, hopeful reflection on enduring through difficult times. The interplay between Taylor's and Justin Vernon's voices creates a sense of harmony and resolution, encapsulating the themes of resilience and hope that run throughout the album.

"Evermore" was also met with critical acclaim and commercial success, debuting at number one on the Billboard 200. The album further solidified Taylor's reputation as a versatile and innovative artist, capable of constantly reinventing herself and her music. The back-to-back releases of "Folklore" and "Evermore" demonstrated Taylor's prolific creativity and her ability to adapt to changing circumstances, even in the midst of a global pandemic.

The "Folklore" and "Evermore" era was a period of introspection and experimentation for Taylor. The albums' stripped-down, folk-inspired sound marked a departure from her previous pop-oriented work, showcasing her versatility as a musician and songwriter. The themes of love, loss, and self-reflection resonated deeply with listeners, offering a sense of comfort and connection during a challenging time.

These albums also highlighted Taylor's ability to collaborate with a diverse range of artists, bringing new perspectives and sounds to her music. The partnerships with Aaron Dessner, Jack Antonoff, and Justin Vernon were particularly significant, as they helped shape the unique sound and atmosphere of "Folklore" and "Evermore." These collaborations underscored the importance of creative partnerships in Taylor's work, allowing her to explore new musical territories and push the boundaries of her artistry.

"Folklore" and "Evermore" represent a pivotal moment in Taylor Swift's career, showcasing her growth as an artist and her willingness to take risks. The albums' introspective themes and innovative sounds have left a lasting impact on her music and her fans, illustrating the power of storytelling and artistic evolution. As Taylor continues to evolve and explore new creative directions, "Folklore" and "Evermore" stand as a testament to her ability to adapt, innovate, and connect with listeners on a profound level.

Chapter 9: Taylor's Version – Reclaiming Her Masters

The issue of artists owning their masters has been a contentious one in the music industry for years, but it reached a crescendo in 2019 when Taylor Swift announced her plan to re-record her first six albums. This bold move was a direct response to the sale of her original masters to Scooter Braun, a manager with whom she had a well-publicized feud. The saga of Taylor's fight to reclaim her masters is a compelling story of artistic integrity, legal battles, and a powerful assertion of control over her own work.

To fully understand the significance of Taylor's decision, it's important to delve into the background of her original record deal with Big Machine Records. When Taylor signed with the label in 2005, she was just 15 years old. The deal included the production and ownership of her masters by Big Machine, a standard practice in the industry but one that would later become a point of contention. Over the years, Taylor expressed her desire to own her masters, but negotiations with Big Machine's founder, Scott Borchetta, did not yield the results she hoped for.

The situation escalated in 2019 when it was announced that Scooter Braun's Ithaca Holdings had acquired Big Machine and, with it, the rights to Taylor's first six albums. Taylor took to social media to express her dismay, accusing Braun of bullying and manipulation. The sale of her masters without her consent was a personal and professional blow, sparking a public debate about artists' rights and ownership.

In response to the sale, Taylor decided to take matters into her own hands. She announced that she would re-record her first six albums, a move that would allow her to regain control over her music. By creating "Taylor's Versions" of her original albums, she aimed to diminish the value of the original masters and offer fans an alternative that she owned outright. This decision was not only a savvy business move but also a statement of empowerment and resilience.

The first of these re-recorded albums, "Fearless (Taylor's Version)," was released in April 2021. The album includes all the tracks from the original "Fearless" album, along with six previously unreleased songs from the vault. Taylor's meticulous attention to detail ensured that the new recordings were faithful to the originals, while subtle changes and enhancements reflected her growth as an artist. "Fearless (Taylor's Version)" was a commercial and critical success, debuting at number one on the Billboard 200 and receiving widespread praise for its quality and authenticity.

The re-recording process was not just about reclaiming her music; it was also an opportunity for Taylor to revisit and reinterpret her past work. In interviews, she described the experience as both nostalgic and cathartic, allowing her to reflect on her journey and the evolution of her artistry. The re-recordings also provided a platform for Taylor to connect with a new generation of fans, many of whom were experiencing her early music for the first time.

"Fearless (Taylor's Version)" was followed by the release of "Red (Taylor's Version)" in November 2021. "Red" was a pivotal album in Taylor's career, marking her transition from country to pop. The re-recorded version includes all the original tracks, plus several new songs from the vault. One of the standout tracks is the 10-minute version of "All Too Well," which had long been a fan favorite. The extended version provided deeper insight into the song's emotional narrative, showcasing Taylor's storytelling prowess.

The release of "Red (Taylor's Version)" was accompanied by a short film for "All Too Well," directed by Taylor herself. The film stars Sadie Sink and Dylan O'Brien, and it visually explores the themes of love, loss, and memory that are central to the song. The short film was widely acclaimed, further cementing "All Too Well" as one of Taylor's most iconic works.

The process of re-recording her albums has also allowed Taylor to address and correct some of the challenges and criticisms of her earlier work. For instance, in "Red (Taylor's Version)," the song "Girl at Home" was reimagined with a more mature and polished production, reflecting Taylor's growth as an artist and producer. These updates provide fans with a fresh perspective on familiar songs, enhancing their appreciation for Taylor's musical evolution.

The re-recording project has had significant implications for the music industry. Taylor's decision to take control of her masters has sparked a broader conversation about artists' rights and the importance of owning one's work. Her actions have inspired other artists to reconsider their own contracts and advocate for greater control over their music. Taylor's fight for her masters has highlighted the need for transparency and fairness in the music industry, paving the way for future generations of artists to navigate their careers with greater autonomy.

Beyond the legal and business aspects, the re-recording project has reinforced Taylor's connection with her fans. The release of "Taylor's Versions" has been celebrated by fans worldwide, who appreciate her dedication to reclaiming her music and her commitment to quality. The re-recordings have also provided a sense of closure and continuity for fans who have followed Taylor's career from the beginning. By revisiting her past work, Taylor has created a bridge between her early music and her current artistry, allowing fans to experience her journey in a new and meaningful way.

The re-recording project is ongoing, with more "Taylor's Versions" expected in the future. Each release is eagerly anticipated by fans, who are excited to hear new interpretations of their favorite songs and discover previously unreleased tracks. The project represents a significant chapter in Taylor's career, showcasing her resilience, creativity, and determination to control her narrative.

In addition to the re-recording project, Taylor has continued to release new music, further solidifying her status as one of the most prolific and innovative artists of her generation. The success of "Folklore" and "Evermore" demonstrated her ability to reinvent herself and explore new musical territories, while the re-recordings have reinforced her connection to her roots. This dual approach has allowed Taylor to maintain a dynamic and evolving career, constantly pushing the boundaries of her artistry while staying true to her core values.

Taylor's journey to reclaim her masters is a testament to her strength and perseverance. It reflects her unwavering commitment to her music and her determination to stand up for her rights as an artist. The re-recording project has not only reshaped her career but also had a lasting impact on the music industry, challenging long-standing practices and advocating for greater fairness and transparency. Taylor's fight for her masters is a powerful example of the importance of owning one's work and the enduring value of artistic integrity.

As Taylor Swift continues to release new "Taylor's Versions" and explore new creative directions, her journey serves as an inspiration to artists and fans alike. Her story is a reminder that taking control of one's narrative and fighting for what is right can lead to profound and lasting change. Taylor's commitment to her music and her fans, combined with her fearless pursuit of artistic and personal growth, has cemented her legacy as one of the most influential and iconic artists of our time.

Chapter 10: Legacy and Influence

Taylor Swift's journey from a teenage country prodigy to a global pop sensation has been nothing short of extraordinary. Her impact on the music industry, pop culture, and the lives of millions of fans around the world is profound and far-reaching. This chapter delves into the legacy and influence of Taylor Swift, examining how her artistic contributions, business acumen, and personal advocacy have left an indelible mark on the world.

One of the most significant aspects of Taylor's legacy is her songwriting. From the very beginning of her career, Taylor has been celebrated for her ability to craft compelling narratives and deeply personal lyrics. Her songs often draw from her own experiences, creating a sense of authenticity and relatability that resonates with listeners. This personal touch has been a hallmark of her music, allowing fans to connect with her on a deeply emotional level. Songs like "Love Story," "All Too Well," and "Cardigan" showcase her talent for storytelling, weaving intricate tales of love, heartbreak, and personal growth.

Taylor's influence as a songwriter extends beyond her own music. She has written songs for other artists, contributing to the success of peers and emerging talents alike. Her collaborations with artists such as Ed Sheeran, Zayn Malik, and Kendrick Lamar demonstrate her versatility and willingness to explore different genres and styles. Taylor's ability to adapt her songwriting to various musical contexts has earned her respect and admiration from fellow musicians and industry professionals.

In addition to her songwriting prowess, Taylor's business acumen has played a crucial role in her legacy. She has consistently taken control of her career, making strategic decisions that have propelled her to new heights. From her early days negotiating a record deal with Big Machine Records to her bold move to re-record her masters, Taylor has demonstrated a keen understanding of the music industry's inner workings. Her decision to leave Big Machine and sign with Republic Records in 2018 was a significant moment in her career, as it granted her greater control over her future recordings.

Taylor's re-recording project, which began with the release of "Fearless (Taylor's Version)" in 2021, is a testament to her determination to reclaim her music and assert her rights as an artist. This move not only allows her to own her masters but also sets a precedent for other artists facing similar challenges. Taylor's fight for ownership has sparked a broader conversation about artists' rights and the importance of fair contracts in the music industry. Her advocacy for artists' control over their work has inspired many to re-evaluate their own contracts and push for greater autonomy.

Taylor's influence extends beyond the music industry to fashion, culture, and social issues. Throughout her career, she has been known for her distinctive style, which has evolved with each era of her music. From the country-inspired dresses and cowboy boots of her early days to the glamorous, high-fashion looks of her "1989" and "Reputation" eras, Taylor's fashion choices have often set trends and inspired fans. Her red carpet appearances and magazine covers have made her a fashion icon, and her ability to reinvent her style has kept her image fresh and relevant.

Taylor's impact on culture is also evident in her use of social media. She has skillfully leveraged platforms like Twitter, Instagram, and Tumblr to connect with fans, share updates, and build a sense of community. Her social media presence is characterized by its authenticity and accessibility, allowing fans to feel a personal connection with her. This direct engagement with her audience has been a key factor in her enduring popularity, as it fosters a sense of loyalty and mutual respect.

In recent years, Taylor has become more vocal about social and political issues, using her platform to advocate for change. Her endorsement of political candidates, support for LGBTQ+ rights, and efforts to raise awareness about issues such as sexual assault and mental health have earned her praise from fans and activists alike. Taylor's willingness to speak out on important issues reflects her growth as a public figure and her commitment to using her influence for good.

One of the most notable examples of Taylor's advocacy is her support for the Equality Act, a proposed piece of legislation aimed at protecting LGBTQ+ individuals from discrimination. In 2019, Taylor wrote a public letter to her senator, urging support for the act, and launched a petition that garnered hundreds of thousands of signatures. Her efforts brought significant attention to the issue and demonstrated her dedication to promoting equality and justice.

Taylor's philanthropic endeavors further underscore her commitment to making a positive impact. Over the years, she has donated millions of dollars to various causes, including education, disaster relief, and public health. She has also supported arts and music education programs, recognizing the importance of nurturing the next generation of artists. Taylor's charitable contributions and advocacy work reflect her belief in giving back to the community and using her resources to help those in need.

Taylor's influence on the next generation of artists is perhaps one of her most enduring legacies. Many young musicians cite her as an inspiration, pointing to her authenticity, resilience, and songwriting skills as qualities they admire. Taylor's willingness to take risks and push boundaries has paved the way for other artists to do the same, encouraging them to stay true to their vision and pursue their passions with confidence.

As Taylor continues to evolve as an artist, her legacy will undoubtedly grow.

Her ability to adapt to changing musical landscapes, connect with fans, and advocate for important causes ensures that she remains a relevant and influential figure in the industry. Taylor's journey is a testament to the power of perseverance, creativity, and authenticity, qualities that will continue to inspire fans and fellow artists for years to come.

Taylor Swift's legacy is multifaceted, encompassing her contributions as a songwriter, her business acumen, her cultural impact, and her advocacy work. Her ability to connect with people through her music, her strategic approach to her career, and her dedication to making a difference in the world have solidified her place as one of the most influential artists of her generation. As we look back on her remarkable journey, it is clear that Taylor Swift's influence will continue to shape the music industry and inspire future generations of artists and fans alike.

Conclusion: The Ever-Evolving Artist

Taylor Swift's career has been a whirlwind of reinvention, from her early days as a teenage country singer to her current status as a global pop icon. Her journey is a testament to her versatility, resilience, and relentless pursuit of artistic growth. This conclusion delves into the key aspects of Taylor's career that have defined her legacy and the lessons that can be drawn from her remarkable evolution.

One of the defining features of Taylor's career is her ability to reinvent herself while maintaining a consistent core identity. Each era of her music is distinct, marked by changes in style, themes, and aesthetics. Yet, despite these shifts, there is a thread of authenticity and personal connection that runs through all her work. This balance between evolution and consistency has allowed Taylor to remain relevant in a constantly changing industry.

Taylor's transition from country to pop was a bold move that could have alienated her original fanbase. However, her careful crafting of "Red" and the full embrace of pop with "1989" showcased her ability to navigate genre boundaries with finesse. This genre fluidity not only expanded her audience but also demonstrated her versatility as an artist. Taylor's willingness to take risks and explore new musical territories has kept her sound fresh and her fans engaged.

Another significant aspect of Taylor's career is her songwriting prowess. From the start, her ability to tell stories through her lyrics set her apart from her peers. Her songs are often deeply personal, drawing from her own experiences and emotions. This authenticity resonates with listeners, creating a sense of intimacy and connection. Taylor's knack for capturing universal themes in her music, such as love, heartbreak, and self-discovery, has made her work relatable to a broad audience.

Taylor's songwriting is not just about personal expression; it also serves as a form of narrative storytelling. Songs like "All Too Well," "Cardigan," and "The Last Great American Dynasty" are mini-narratives, each with its own characters, settings, and plots. This narrative approach adds depth to her music, inviting listeners to immerse themselves in the stories she tells. Taylor's ability to weave intricate tales within her songs is a testament to her creativity and literary sensibility.

In addition to her artistic achievements, Taylor's business acumen has played a crucial role in her success. Her decision to leave Big Machine Records and sign with Republic Records was a strategic move that gave her greater control over her music. The subsequent re-recording of her early albums, starting with "Fearless (Taylor's Version)," was a masterstroke. This project not only allowed her to reclaim her masters but also revitalized her early work for a new generation of fans. Taylor's savvy understanding of the music industry and her assertiveness in business matters have been key to her longevity and influence.

Taylor's use of social media has also been instrumental in her career. From her early engagement with fans on MySpace to her current presence on platforms like Instagram and Twitter, Taylor has consistently used social media to connect with her audience. Her posts are often personal and candid, giving fans a glimpse into her life and thoughts. This direct line of communication fosters a sense of loyalty and community among her followers. Taylor's adept use of social media has allowed her to stay connected with her fanbase and adapt to the digital age of music promotion.

Taylor's influence extends beyond music to fashion and culture. Her style evolution—from the cowboy boots and sundresses of her country days to the chic, high-fashion looks of her pop eras—has made her a fashion icon. Her red carpet appearances and magazine covers are closely watched and often set trends. Taylor's ability to reinvent her image with each album release keeps her visually fresh and relevant, contributing to her overall appeal and impact on popular culture.

In recent years, Taylor has become more outspoken on social and political issues. Her public endorsement of political candidates, support for LGBTQ+ rights, and advocacy for artists' rights have added another dimension to her public persona. Taylor's willingness to use her platform for activism reflects her growth as a public figure and her commitment to making a positive impact. Her advocacy efforts have resonated with fans and brought attention to important issues, highlighting the role of artists as influencers in society.

Taylor's philanthropy further underscores her dedication to making a differ-ence. She has donated millions to various causes, including disaster relief, education, and public health. Her support for arts and music education programs demonstrates her commitment to nurturing future generations of artists. Taylor's charitable efforts reflect her belief in giving back to the community and using her success to benefit others.

The impact of Taylor Swift's career on the music industry is profound. She has challenged industry norms, advocated for artists' rights, and set new standards for creative control and business acumen. Her ability to navigate the complexities of fame, maintain artistic integrity, and evolve with the times has made her a model for aspiring musicians. Taylor's influence is evident in the careers of countless young artists who cite her as an inspiration and role model.

Taylor's journey also offers valuable lessons in resilience and perseverance. She has faced numerous challenges, from public feuds and media scrutiny to personal setbacks. Yet, she has consistently emerged stronger, using adversity as fuel for her creative endeavors. Taylor's ability to turn obstacles into opportunities and maintain her focus on her artistic vision is a testament to her strength and determination.

As Taylor continues to evolve, her legacy will undoubtedly grow. Her contributions to music, culture, and society have left an indelible mark, and her influence will be felt for years to come. Taylor Swift's story is one of continuous reinvention, artistic exploration, and unwavering authenticity. Her journey serves as an inspiration to artists and fans alike, illustrating the power of staying true to oneself and pursuing one's passions with courage and creativity.

Taylor Swift's career is a testament to the transformative power of music and the enduring impact of an artist who dares to innovate, inspire, and connect. Her legacy is not just in the songs she has written or the records she has sold, but in the hearts and minds of the millions of people she has touched with her music and her message. As she continues to create, advocate, and evolve, Taylor Swift remains a beacon of artistic excellence and a symbol of the ever-changing landscape of the music industry.

Made in United States
Troutdale, OR
12/15/2024

26626479R00037